MY LIFE MAP

A Journal to Help You Shape Your Future

BY KATE AND DAVID MARSHALL

GOTHAM BOOKS

GOTHAM BOOKS
Published by Penguin Group (USA) Inc.
375 Hudson Street, New York, New York 10014, U.S.A.
Penguin Group (Canada), 90 Eglinton Avenue East, Suite 700, Toronto, Ontario M4P 2Y3, Canada
(a division of Pearson Penguin Canada Inc.); Penguin Books Ltd, 80 Strand, London WC2R 0RL, England;
Penguin Ireland, 25 St Stephen's Green, Dublin 2, Ireland (a division of Penguin Books Ltd); Penguin Group (Australia),
250 Camberwell Road, Camberwell, Victoria 3124, Australia (a division of Pearson Australia Group Pty Ltd);
Penguin Books India Pvt Ltd, 11 Community Centre, Panchsheel Park, New Delhi—110 017, India; Penguin Group (NZ),
67 Apollo Drive, Rosedale, Auckland 0632, New Zealand (a division of Pearson New Zealand Ltd);
Penguin Books (South Africa) (Pty) Ltd, 24 Sturdee Avenue, Rosebank, Johannesburg 2196, South Africa

Penguin Books Ltd, Registered Offices: 80 Strand, London WC2R 0RL, England

Published by Gotham Books, a member of Penguin Group (USA) Inc.

First printing, November 2012
10   9   8   7   6   5   4   3   2   1

LIBRARY OF CONGRESS CATALOGING-IN-PUBLICATION DATA
Marshall, Kate, 1959–
    My life map : a journal to help you shape your future / by Kate and David Marshall.
        p.   cm.
    Includes bibliographical references.
    ISBN 978-1-592-40784-2 (pbk.)
    1. Conduct of life.   2. Goal (Psychology)   I. Marshall, David, 1956–   II. Title.
    BJ1589.M27 2012
    158.1—dc23
    2012009515

Printed in the United States of America
Set in Archer, with display in Gotham
Designed by BTDNYC

ALWAYS LEARNING   PEARSON

CONTENTS

INTRODUCTION

"If you don't know where you're going, any road will take you there."

—LEWIS CARROLL

*"Your time is limited, so don't waste it living someone else's life. . . .
Don't let the noise of others' opinions drown out your own inner voice. . . .
[H]ave the courage to follow your heart and intuition."*

—STEVE JOBS, STANFORD UNIVERSITY
COMMENCEMENT ADDRESS

OUR JOB IN LIFE is not so much to *find* ourselves as it is to *create* ourselves. What will you create? How do you want to be remembered? What will your legacy be? *My Life Map* helps you create direction, flow, and meaning to your journey.

Before saying that life mapping is too hard or that your future is too uncertain to make any meaningful plans, we encourage you to give this process a chance. We often played The Game of Life when we were young; did you? Imagine how fun the game would be if you got to make up all your own career, house, and family cards. That's what you will be doing in this book.

A traditional autobiography tells the life story as it already happened. *My Life Map* is different. It reviews your past and present, and imagines the life stories you hope to experience in the future. No matter what stage of life you are in now, it can be helpful to draw a visual road map of your yesterdays and tomorrows in major areas such as work, service, learning, family, friends, and playing. Mapping out the past highlights patterns you may not have noticed before. Seeing the blank years ahead in the Life Map offers a chance to pause and reflect on your future, and encourages you to be intentional about how your story unfolds.

We're confident that the guidance and prompting questions this book offers will make it much easier and, dare we say, more *fun*, than you think. You really can do this. Even if you are not prone to introspection of this kind, we trust that *My Life Map* will help you to envision your medium- and long-term goals with more clarity, and that this clarity will lead to actions now that build toward the future you want.

—KATE AND DAVID MARSHALL

1. HOW TO USE THIS BOOK
Tips and Sample Maps

WHY MAP YOUR LIFE?

"It is never too late to be who you might have been."

—GEORGE ELIOT

"The clearer you can be about your long-term future, the more rapidly you will attract the people and circumstances into your life to help make that future a reality."

—BRIAN TRACY, *GOALS!*

WHY MAP YOUR LIFE? The goal of life mapping is a meaningful and fulfilled life. Seeing your entire life on one map helps you to live with intention and purpose, and increases the chances that you will achieve your goals. If you develop and organize your thoughts into a visual picture of your hopes and dreams, you are not only more likely to actively work toward them, but you will also be better prepared to recognize and take advantage of unexpected opportunities that may come along.

Why is it important to view your whole life from start to finish? Why not just create a future map? Seeing the whole life—past, present, and future—offers an important perspective in shaping the future you want. By seeing patterns and turning points in your past, you can see what has and hasn't worked well so far. You may acknowledge, accept, and honor what has come before, and then move on.

If this sort of life planning is already familiar to you—you have a firm understanding of your past and a clear picture of your goals for all main areas of your life—you may not need to do all the warm-up material in this book. For you, glancing at the sample Whole-Life Maps on pages 14–21 and choosing just the exercises in the "Reflecting on Your Past and Present" and "Your Future" chapters that cover new ground for you may be enough to get you going on your own maps. However, if it has been a while since you've allowed yourself to calmly reflect and dream, linger a while over the questions posed in the next few chapters. You may be surprised by how much deeper they will take you.

IMPORTANT: If the idea of long-term planning terrifies you, and it might, take a deep breath. You are not being asked to make irrevocable decisions here, or to let go of spontaneity in your life. You will not be a failure if what you write in this book does not come true. This book is simply a dialogue with yourself. If you're still feeling anxious, pretend you are using the Life Maps to sketch the life story of a character in a novel you are writing. Like many novelists, you create a character who resembles you and whom you care deeply about. You want the very best for this person, so the life story you tell is one which you would find satisfying, too.

When should you start mapping your life? Start at any time, at any age, whether you're in your twenties or in midlife contemplating the second half of life. Life mapping is particularly helpful when:

→ **You're just starting out and have an entire life to plan**

→ **You have major decisions ahead, such as:**
   →What should I do after graduation?
   →Should I have children? When?
   →Am I too old for graduate school?
   →What's the best path to the job I want?
   →Should I say yes to this job, project, or other opportunity?
   →When should I retire?

→ **You are facing a transition time, such as:**
   →The beginning of a life partnership (marriage)
   →The end of a life partnership (divorce, death)
   →Graduating from school
   →Babies coming into your life or grown children leaving it
   →Adjusting to a challenging health, personal, or family circumstance
   →Recovering from a condition or attitude that used to limit you
   →Moving to a new city
   →Going back to work after raising a family
   →An unexpected job loss or change
   →Retiring from work

If you are filling these maps out in your twenties or thirties, they will be mostly the story of your future. Your past is brief. You've got a lot of future to work with. The Ten-Year Map may feel long term enough for you, but push yourself to go all the way in the Whole-Life Map. In your Whole-Life Map, you have the chance to write down the jobs you imagine having in your life. You can write down all the places you hope to live in, and when. You can record when you hope to marry or have children. You can also write down the year you expect to retire and the year you imagine dying.

If you are in your middle years, you have more of the past to record. You will have the chance to reflect on your life thus far. Has it gone the way you thought it would? If not, how so? Have there been unfulfilled dreams for your family, education, or work lives? Why did your path meander in unintended ways? If you are happy with how things have turned out, to what do you attribute your good fortune? Was it meeting and falling in love with your soul mate that made the difference? Or raising your children? Or landing the right job? Even in the most satisfying of lives, there are bound to have been some roads that led to dead ends. What changes do you want to make to lead your life in a more meaningful and satisfying direction? Now is the time to think about what you want to do with the time you have left.

Which Maps, When?

There is no wrong way to do these maps—whatever works for *you* is the right way. The first five chapters offer tips, warm-up exercises, and clarifying questions that can deepen your experience and result in plans that are in tune with your true desires. They cover why and when life mapping is helpful. They offer exercises to give you insights into what is important to you and to help you start identifying how you want your future to look. They lead you through how to fill out your Life Maps—possible topics, how much detail, summarizing and naming chapters, and tips on formatting.

There are three kinds of maps in this book:

1. **Subject Map:** a set of six maps, each covering one aspect of your life (Family, Friends, Learning, Work, Service, Playing) over the next ten years (pages 50–73).
2. **Ten-Year Map:** one map covering all aspects of your life over the next ten years (pages 74–77).
3. **Whole-Life Map:** one map covering all aspects of your life over your whole life span, from birth to death (pages 78–79).

This book presents the maps in the above order, with the smaller picture maps first, and builds to the biggest picture: first the trees, then the forest. This order lets you start with more immediate dreams that may already be in the works. This may feel more comfortable to you than jumping into a longer-term vision. It allows you to start with certain themes or parts of your life that you may have already done some thinking about, such as your work, play, or family life. Start with the ten-year Subject Map covering the area most familiar or most important to you. If you are a Bottom-Up Thinker, Thematic Thinker, or are just not comfortable jumping into longer-term planning right away, use this order.

If this order does not feel right to you, feel free to flip it around: draw the forest first, then the trees. With this order, you develop your long-term vision first in the Whole-Life Map, then use the full Ten-Year Map to sketch your medium-term goals and steps that move you toward your longer-term visions, and then do the Subject Maps to flesh out more detailed plans for each part of your life (family, friends, work, etc.). If you are a Top-Down Thinker, or you already know what your long-term dreams are but not necessarily how to get there, you might prefer this order. Also consider starting with the Whole-Life Map if you think it likely that you will run out of steam if it takes too long to get there—the full life map is important.

In any case, start by writing about your past—the years you have already lived—and your present on the Whole-Life Map, then move on to the future map of your choice.

IF YOU ARE A:	DO THE MAPS IN THIS ORDER:
BOTTOM-UP THINKER— You prefer to start with what you know, then build toward a broader vision.	1. The past and present in your Whole-Life Map 2. Subject Maps (any order) 3. Ten-Year Map 4. The future in your Whole-Life Map
THEMATIC THINKER— You prefer to think about one thing at a time, from start to finish.	One subject at a time, until all maps are full. Start with the subject that is easiest or matters most to you. 1. The _____ (Work or other subject) row in your Whole-Life Map—past and present 2. _____ Subject Map 3. The _____ row in your Ten-Year Map 4. The _____ row in your Whole-Life Map—future 5. Start again with a new subject (e.g. Playing)
TOP-DOWN THINKER— You prefer to get the long-term, big picture first, then work out the details.	1. The past and present in your Whole-Life Map 2. The future in your Whole-Life Map 3. Ten-Year Map 4. Subject Maps (any order)
RANDOM THINKER— You are guided by intuition and prefer to sketch things out as they occur to you and let the whole picture unfold.	Skim the maps and start filling them out in bits and pieces whenever, wherever you are inspired to do so.

GENERAL MAPPING TIPS

 Summarize

Resist the temptation to write a lot of detail about your past on your maps. Not only is there not enough room for it, but you will learn more about key trends in your life by looking at the big picture. Journal your thoughts on the lines provided in this book or in a side notebook before summarizing them in the maps.

Name Themes

A big part of life mapping is identifying and naming themes in your life, both in your past and your future. Summarizing or naming segments will lead you to clearer takeaways from your maps. If you moved around in your twenties, rather than list every town you lived in in the Place row, you could simply name that time "exploring the world," "searching for new community," or "wandering aimlessly." Likewise, if you frequently changed jobs until you found the right career path, you might name that period "exploring my options" or "I once was lost . . ." Or name the dominant feeling from that period "content," "confused," or "in love." See the Sample Whole-Life Maps for more examples of naming.

Use Images

When filling out your map, consider using symbols, drawings, or other visual prompts as well as words to depict events. Draw them yourself or use stickers or clip art. A visual map will be easier to see patterns in than a map dense with text. Visual images of your future may also be more motivating and stay with you longer.

 *Use Pencil (Not Pen) and a Ruler*

Give yourself the freedom to try things out—sketch out a plan and tweak it or completely redo it—until you're happy with it. Unless you naturally draw straight lines, use a ruler to divide your past from your future and to create chapters on your Life Map. (You'll learn about chapters on page 39.)

Electronic Option

You may prefer to work on your maps on your computer in a word processing, graphics, or spreadsheet program. If so, create your own maps using those presented here as a guide, or go to www.marshallbooks.net for a starter set (use code XM4U2MLM). After you finish your electronic versions, print them and paste them in the pages of *My Life Map* or post them where you can see them every day.

Buddy System

Consider pairing up with your life partner or a trusted friend to talk through the exercises together. Explain your finished maps to each other and support each other's dreams as you move forward.

Pace Yourself

Finally, there are a *lot* of exercises and maps offered in this journal. Pace yourself. Don't let yourself get overwhelmed—it is not an all or nothing deal. It's okay to leave some maps partly or fully blank. You might have a lot to write about family but not work or play, or the other way around. Do as many exercises and maps as are helpful to you—no more, no less.

SAMPLE WHOLE-LIFE MAPS

The next eight pages show how Whole-Life Maps can look when finished. The purely fictitious characters of Lucy, Kyle, Karen, and Alex filled out their pasts as they happened and their futures as they envision them.

SAMPLE WHOLE-LIFE MAP—LUCY (AGE 23)

Lucy has just graduated from college with a degree in psychology and is figuring out her next steps. She's enjoying her temp job in a doctor's office and her volunteer work in a hospice. In the future, she sees herself raising a family and staying active in cheerleading

← PAST — — — — — — — PRESENT — — — — — —

Name: Lucy	Current Age (23)	Date: Jan. 1, 2013
YEARS	1989–2009	2010–2019	2020–2029
AGE	0–20	21–30	31–40
CHAPTER	FINDING MYSELF		SERVING
PLACE	Tampa Tallahassee	Gainesville . . .	
FAMILY	X X brother Grampa born died	♡ find love	⚭ marry 👣 baby 1 👣 baby 2 x x
FRIENDS	BFF = Becky . . . Cheerleading . . . Kappa girls . . .	+ new work friends	
LEARNING	BS Psych FSU	BS Nursing U of FL	cooking parenting
WORK	Babysitting Dr. K's	office	pediatric nurse! . . . full-time part-time . . .
SERVICE	hospice volunteer . . .	Vote!	📢 cheerleading coach
PLAYING	Cheerleading Shopping	Dance Nights	x Broadway Musical 30th Birthday
OTHER	X house fire		🏠 HOME buy house with yard

and dance. She thinks a career in nursing would be satisfying and also give her the flexibility she needs to work part-time while her future kids are young. Her dream trip would be to visit France with someone she loves. A visual person, Lucy decorated her map with drawings, printed it out, and posted it on her home bulletin board as a reminder.

FUTURE ⟶

LIFE TITLE: Dancing My Way Thru Life			
2030–2039	2040–2049	2050–2059	2060–94
41-50	**51-60**	**61-70**	**71-105**
OTHERS		RELAXING	

retire at the beach— ☀
Pensacola?

parenting!!   X   X
child 1 college   child 2 college   🌹
          kids leave!!   50th Anniversary!

+ parenting friends   + theater friends

singing   learn French   keep learning!
📖

full-time
nursing (new specialty?)   X
🩹   retire

volunteer in kids'   local theater troupe
schools/scouts/other   care for Mom and Dad   🎭

🎵 Dancing for exercise
kid activities   🗼 vacation in France   RV travel

$ smart
investments   inheritance—buy RV

SAMPLE WHOLE-LIFE MAP—KYLE (AGE 35)

Kyle is a smart, ambitious young man. His career in law pays for his passion for travel. His goal is to work hard to make partner in his new firm and then retire early enough to pursue his many interests and goals: write a book, compete on *Jeopardy!* (or in a

Name: **Kyle**	Date: 1/1/2013					Current age (35)
YEARS	1978–1998			1999–2008		2009–2018
AGE	0–20			21–30		31–40
CHAPTER	P l a y			S t a n d i n g U p F o r t h e		
PLACE	MA RI New Jersey CT (Jr Yr Peru)			NYC D.C....		
FAMILY	Suburban comforts		Divorce divides us		Amy, right girlfriend ...	Family makes peace Get a dog
FRIENDS	Good Freaks Fun Nerds		too busy	Fellow Misfits — roommates and wrong girlfriends		
LEARNING	College-prep	Wes-leyan Univ. B.A. Film	NYU Law School J.D.	Relationships ... Gardening ...		
WORK	English Tutor		JBC&D Assoc.	BN&R Sr. Assoc. conflict → compatible cut throat → teamwork		x Jr. Partner (or change firms)
SERVICE	Earth Club		park cleanup	2% to charity ...		8% to charity ...
PLAYING	YES! Make films Taiko Poetry			NO (postponing play) ...		....
OTHER		Asia trip		Brazil trip Gained weight		China trip School loans paid off

crossword competition), and travel. A child of an ugly divorce, Kyle is not sure he wants to marry and have children, but he does want to have a committed love partner in his life. He dreams of an active retirement, with service adventures such as an overseas Peace Corps assignment, and expects to have lots of stories to tell at his fiftieth college reunion.

— — FUTURE — — — — — — — — — — — — — — — — →

LIFE TITLE: He Came, He Saw, He Gave			
2019–2028	2029–2038	2039–2048	2049–?
41–50	51–60	61–70	71–__
Little Guy		World Citizen	

Consider AZ or CA when weary of winters . . .   Some distant land

Settled happily with partner . . .
x
Cousin reunion

Cool people who challenge and excite me
(from both in/out work)   At least half are younger than I

x
writing class
                        x
                Big Brain Challenge   Teaching
                (*Jeopardy!* crossword championship)   Foreign Language
                                                          World Religions (and pick one)

        x   x   x
    Equity Partner!   part-time law   retire
        x   x   x
    . . . write book   . . . publish book   . . . NYT bestseller!

                                                          Peace
                                                          Corps!
community garden   ESL Tutor
                pro bono law cases   Master Gardener

                                                              x
                YES, play a LOT again!   50th college reunion
                Read/write biographies, invent, putter, tinker . . .

With Dad—
Norway trip   India trip   Dude ranch trip   Ireland trip
        Lose 10+ pounds   Financially secure

After being a full-time mom and volunteer at her kids' schools for many years, it suddenly hit Karen that she would soon be facing an empty nest. It terrified her that she had no idea what that would look like for her. Her before-children job was unfulfilling, and she wants a positive work experience that more closely matches her skills and interests.

← PAST —

Name: **Karen**			Date: Jan. 1, 2013
YEARS	1965–1985	1986–1995	1996–2005
AGE	0–20	21–30	31–40
CHAPTER	SMALL-TOWN GIRL		CARING FOR
PLACE	Akron Family home FRIENDLY	Chicago apt downtown BUSY	Minneapolis . . . new home . . . SUPPORTIVE . . .
FAMILY	Mom, Dad, Andy, Susan strict but loving FIRST FAMILY	Jerry! +Amber +Nick (+Curly) CREATE NEW FAMILY	
FRIENDS	Neighborhood Follower CLOSE-KNIT	? LONELY	from school activities MANY CASUAL FRIENDS . . .
LEARNING	Values, work ethic Crafting . . . ARTISTIC	banking ANALYTIC	homemaking . . . patience . . . CREATIVE
WORK	Office Assistant	Mortgage Bank BAD FIT	Stay-at-Home Mom . . . GOOD FIT . . .
SERVICE	Scouting	Counsel Andy	Raise kids . . . Room parent Help Dad
PLAYING	art . . . piano . . .	stamping . . . fishing at Lake Vermilion . . .	quilting . . . scrapbooking . . .
OTHER HAPPINESS FACTOR	☺(family)	☹(friends, work)	☺(new family) ☹ (Dad's death)

In her vision of the future, Karen is surrounded by beloved craft projects, an entrepreneurial award, and fun times with her husband and grandchildren. Her breakthrough idea is to get a job in school administration with people she knows through her volunteer work and, best of all, to start and develop an online craft business.

PRESENT — FUTURE →

LIFE TITLE: H a v i n g I t A l l (B u t N o t A l l a t O n c e)

Current age (48)

2006–2015	2016–2025	2026–2035	2036–2050
41-50	51-60	61-70	71-85
OTHERS	CARING FOR MYSELF— CRAFTING QUEEN		
	1. Minneapolis home + 2. Cabin @ Lake Vermilion RELAXING . . .		
LAUNCH KIDS	Kids to college EMPTY NEST!	Jerry retires A COUPLE AGAIN	GRANDPARENTING
Jerry's office	Girls' weekends Leader FEWER, DEEPER FRIENDSHIPS		
gratitude ORGANIZED	Computers Office admin.	Own business ENTREPRENEURIAL	
	1. School District office 2. Online craft co. HEARTFELT . . .	Retire from school Craft business goes public!	
PTA Treasurer	Help Mom . . .	Support Food Bank Help Aunt Sue . . .	
knitting/crocheting . . . Scrabble . . .	making candles/felting . . .	all kinds of crafting!	
☹(Mom's health)	☺(new work) ☹(empty nest)	☺(cabin)	☺(biz success)

SAMPLE WHOLE-LIFE MAP—ALEX (AGE 62)

Alex calls himself "The Comeback Kid." Born in East Germany, his immediate family made it to West Germany in 1960, just before the Berlin Wall went up. He immigrated to California, worked as an engineer, and married. After some happy years—reuniting with lost relatives from East Germany, becoming a U.S. citizen, and marrying—the last decade

← PAST —

Name: Alex			Date: 1/1/2013	
YEARS	1951–1971		1972–1981	1982–1991
AGE	0–20		21–30	31–40
CHAPTER	DEUTSCHLAND		BECOMING AN AMERICAN	
PLACE	DDR— East Germany	GDR—West Germany Munich TU Berlin	San Francisco Bay Area Apt in SF, CA	House in Oakland, CA
FAMILY	United Family	Divided Family— East/West	Opa visit	Marry Anna + stepson Tonio ♡
FRIENDS	Fritz	Teammates— Karl, Philip, Max	Coworkers— Mark, Jason Max died	Neighbors— Andersons
LEARNING		English B.S. Civil Engineering	☆ Astronomy	
WORK		Summers— AWL, AG	CAL TRANS— Transportation Planning . . .	
SERVICE	help Oma		unoffical B&B(!) neighborhood handyman	AIDS Walk x 4
PLAYING	soccer	Soccer Club	Ski Tour NASA	49er tickets
OTHER	1961– Berlin Wall		☺ U.S. Citizen!! ☺ German Reunification!	

or so has been tough. A back injury left him unable to work for a period. He was divorced, then laid off. Undaunted, Alex has drawn strength from his faith. He develops a plan in his map to find work as a consultant and to teach at a junior college. He envisions meeting a new love through church activities and taking her on a trip to meet his extended family in Germany.

—— —— —— —— —— —— —— PRESENT —— —— —— FUTURE —— —→

LIFE TITLE: The Comeback Kid

↓ Current age (62)

1992–2001	2002–2011	2012–2021	2022–?
41–50	**51–60**	**61–70**	**71–__**
I ONCE WAS LOST		BUT THEN WAS FOUND	
San Francisco Bay Area Town house in Fremont, CA		3 BR house with a pool, near work and restaurants	
Divorce ☹ Internet matchmaking (no matches) Visit lost relatives in Germany		Find soul mate at church Marry ♡ Introduce new wife to relatives in Germany	
Bible study mates— Susan, Eric Godfather to Jacob		Family and church friends	
Bible study Yoga		Continued Bible study Classical music	
CAL TRANS— Rail Planning X Laid off Job Hunt I- Disability -I		Part-time transportation consultant Math and Science Teacher at Community College	
H.S. Robotics Club Mentor		Church committees on hunger, health	
Germany trip Movies		49er tickets Germany trip	
⚡ Back Injury—Physical Therapy		Healthy back Exercise I enjoy	

2. YOUR PAST

"To look to the future we must first look back upon the past.
That is where the seeds of the future were planted."

—ALBERT EINSTEIN

Warm-Up Questions

Place: What was your favorite room in the home you grew up in? Why?

_____

_____

Family: List the first words you think of to describe your family when you were young.

_____

_____

Friends: Who were your best friends in high school? How did you meet?

_____

_____

Learning: Who was one of your most memorable teachers? Why?

_____

_____

Work: When you were young, what did you want to be when you grew up? Why?

_____

_____

Service: Name a time when you felt good for helping someone or something.

_____

_____

Playing: What were your favorite games or play things as a kid?

_____

_____

Writing Your Past in Your Whole-Life Map

First set up your Whole-Life Map on pages 78–79 with your ages and years across the top, as follows:

Headers: Name, today's date (leave the Life Title for later).

Years and Age: Write the years that span each decade, from your birth to old age. (Note that the first column represents your first twenty years and the rest of the columns show ten years each. You could also renumber the columns 0–10, 11–20, 21–30, 31–40, 41–50, 51–60, 61–__.) Now find your current age and draw a vertical line from the very top to the very bottom of the chart to separate your past from your future. Use a ruler if desired.

Chapters: Leave this row blank for now. (You will be writing in this row after the past and present years are fleshed out and you have reflected on them in Chapter 4, "Reflecting on Your Past and Present.")

Now ask yourself the following questions about your past. Make notes on these pages or in a side notebook, then summarize the most important aspects of your notes in the Whole-Life Map on pages 78–79. Refer back to the Sample Whole-Life Maps on pages 14–21 for ways to represent your past on the map.

Place: From birth to now, write down where you have lived so far. You can record cities, states, regions, countries, or summarize them. If you've moved around a lot, you can try to squeeze them all in on the map, or simply write themes such as "East Coast," "So Many Suburbs," or "World Traveler."

_____

_____

_____

_____

Family: This could include names of family members and pets; noteworthy births, deaths, marriages, divorces; the characteristics (loving, chaotic, tense) or the circumstances (poor, combined, foster) of your family at the time. If you considered a particular romantic partner to be your family—legally or not—then include that relationship here. Or put it in the Friends row.

_____

_____

_____

_____

Friends: In this row, you could write the names of special friends; categorize your "community" (teammates, coworkers, a common interest, ethnic or religious group);

how you knew them (camp, school, work); how you felt about your social life at the time (leader, close-knit, loner, bullied); or any other way to describe your community or the role that friends had in your life. Romantic attachments (or breakups) could go here in the Friends row or in the Family row above.

_____

_____

_____

_____

Learning: This can be both subjects you studied and degrees you earned in formal settings, as well as things you learned in work (marketing, customer service, forklifts, time management) and in life through hobbies, activities, and independent learning (golf, spirituality, astronomy, decision-making, cooking, humility). It could also include what you considered your "purpose" at the time (becoming a writer, healing, parenting, finding faith).

_____

_____

_____

_____

Work: You can simply list the names of employers, the kinds of jobs or fields you worked in (retail, self-employed, design) or you can write how you experienced your work (bouncing around, labor of love, selling out, climbing the ladder). Other personal missions could go here, too (fighting a health challenge, getting sober). What successes or challenges were there?

_____

_____

_____

_____

Service: This is about service to others. What responsibilities or missions have been meaningful to you? Think about all you have done for your family, your local community, and the world at large: caring for children or an elder, helping a friend in need, serving on a committee, volunteering, donating to or supporting a cause, or being politically engaged. (It is okay if this overlaps with other sections, such as Family or Work.)

_____

_____

_____

_____

Playing: What did you like to do when you weren't in class or working? Recall your hobbies, sports activities, travel, and other fun experiences that didn't seem like work. What were your favorite indoor and outdoor activities? What did you most enjoy or excel at?

_____

_____

_____

_____

Other: Use this space for any other noteworthy events, milestones, or periods. Consider using it to record:

- the emotional highs and lows in your life. Pinpoint highs and lows with X's or emoticons, or draw them as a continuous line going up and down like the results of an EKG heart test
- financial highlights, lowlights, or milestones (salaries, student loans paid, mortgage paid, personal bankruptcy, or your first $ __ saved)
- physical or mental health challenges you faced
- major events in the world that affected you then (economic recession, war, election, new law, natural disaster)

- cultural trends that influenced you (music, movies, or books that touched you; people you looked up to; diet or fitness trends)
- other significant events

_____

_____

_____

_____

Now record the highlights of your past in your Whole-Life Map on pages 78–79, then return to the next chapter, "Your Present."

3. YOUR PRESENT

"The present is the ever moving shadow that divides yesterday from tomorrow. In that lies hope."

—FRANK LLOYD WRIGHT, *THE LIVING CITY*

"The past empowers the present, and the sweeping footsteps leading to this present mark the pathways to the future."

—MARY CATHERINE BATESON

MAKE SURE YOU HAVE filled in your Whole-Life Map all the way up to today. Use the following prompts to be sure that it includes all the major points of what is happening in your life now. This will be your starting point for creating your future.

Place: How would you describe where you are living now (location, community, house or apartment, with whom, rent/own, style, ambiance, or other description)?

_____

_____

_____

Family: How would you describe your family now (family members, marital status, health of your relationships, or other description)?

_____

_____

_____

Friends: How would you characterize your friendships now (who your friends are, quantity or quality of friendships, status of your dating life, or other characterizations)?

_____

_____

_____

Learning: What are you learning or exploring now, either in school, at work, or in your personal life? Are you in training or working toward a degree?

_____

_____

_____

Work: What is happening in your work life right now (field, employer, position, duties, coworkers, boss, likes/dislikes, rewards)?

_____

_____

_____

Service: Who or what are you trying to help or support now, with thoughts, words, or deeds (individuals, organizations, causes)?

_____

_____

_____

Playing: What do you do for fun now (hobbies, interests, physical or mental play, entertainment, how often you make time for play)?

_____

_____

_____

_____

Other: What else important is happening in your life now (health, financial or legal situation, community or neighborhood issue, or other)?

_____

_____

_____

4. REFLECTING ON YOUR PAST AND PRESENT

Where You Have Been, Where You Are Now

"Turn your wounds into wisdom."

—OPRAH WINFREY

"Study the past if you would divine the future."

—CONFUCIUS

NOW THAT YOU HAVE recorded your past and present on the Whole-Life Map, take some time to reflect on where you have been and where you are now in life before moving on to your future.

Mementos

What memento have you saved from your past that gives you pleasure or has special meaning to you now?

_____

_____

_____

_____

Strengths

List five talents, abilities, or gifts that you have enjoyed developing and using in your life now or in the past (physical, intellectual, interpersonal, creative, moral):

STRENGTHS
1.
2.
3.
4.
5.

Top-10 Significant Events

What have been the most significant events and milestones in your life so far (graduations, romances begun or ended, major illness, new job, births, moves, discovery of a talent, and other successes, struggles, turning points, major decisions, and discoveries)? List them here:

TOP-10 SIGNIFICANT EVENTS
1.
2.
3.
4.
5.
6.
7.
8.
9.
10.

Emotional Highs and Lows

Looking back, what were the emotional high and low points of your life so far? These may be the same as your significant events, but not necessarily. Emotional highs may include a major event such as graduating from college, but also the everyday happiness of living by the beach for a few years. Emotional lows could be dramatic events such as divorce or death of a loved one, but also periods of loneliness, stress, or uncertainty.

TOP-5 EMOTIONAL HIGHS OR LOWS	
← Low	High →
1.	
2.	
3.	
4.	
5.	

As you wrote about your life until now, did you find yourself missing anything from your past? What (if anything) would you like to bring back into your life?

_____

_____

_____

_____

Looking back, has anything held you back from being happy and fulfilled (money, health, attitude, relationships, responsibilities)? How could you change that limitation or how it affects you in the future?

_____

_____

_____

_____

What are you most grateful for in your present life?

_____

_____

_____

_____

Grade yourself on these aspects of your life (E=Excellent, G=Good, S=Satisfactory, U=Unsatisfactory, N/A):

_____ Work   _____ Friends

_____ Serving Others   _____ Playing

_____ Formal Learning   _____ Finances

_____ Informal Learning   _____ Home/Place

_____ Love Life   _____ Physical Health

_____ Immediate Family   _____ Overall Well-Being

_____ Extended Family

Which of these grades are you most proud of? _____

_____

_____

Why do you think those areas are going well for you (luck, perseverance, family support, faith, talent, other)? _____

_____

_____

_____

Which areas do you most want to improve? _____

_____

_____

_____

What aspect of your life tends to drive your happiness (up or down): family, friends, work, service, playing, or other? This insight may help focus your vision for a happy future.

_____

_____

_____

Do you see any other patterns, themes, or lessons as you look at your past and present laid out on your Whole-Life Map?

_____

_____

_____

Responsibilities

What are your top three responsibilities now (caring for children or an elder parent, making money, finishing school, getting healthy, leading a team)?

1.

2.

3.

Decisions

What are the three biggest decisions facing you right now? State your question in just a few words ("Should I break up with _____?," "Which classes should I take?," "Should I apply for a _____ job?," "Where should I live?," "Should I get pregnant now?").

1.

2.

3.

Which Box?

What in your current life do you want to keep and what do you want to change in the next five to ten years (house, job, hobby, person, attitude, talent, health habit, or condition)? List them here in the Keep or Change boxes:

KEEP:	CHANGE:

Naming Your Life Chapters

Now that you have reflected on your Past and Present, you are ready to name your past chapters. There is a row toward the top of the Whole-Life Map and the Ten-Year Map labeled "Chapter." This is where you summarize a period of time with a unifying theme. Name your past chapters now, as explained below, and your future chapters later, after mapping your future.

Create Chapters: Look for patterns, themes, trends, and ways to group years together into chapters. Some chapters may be short and others may span decades. Summarize as much as possible; try not to divide your life into so many chapters that you no longer see the major themes of your life. Draw vertical lines to divide the Chapter row into your themes. Use the Sample Whole-Life Maps for ideas.

Name Chapters: Why did you group those years together? How would you describe that era? Come up with a catchy title for each chapter. Was it a happy time ("Family Fun on the Farm," "Business Takes Off")? Was it a difficult time that you want to reframe in a positive light ("Building Years," "Learning Life Lessons"), or do you want to call it like it was ("My Dirty Rotten Childhood," "Lonely Days")?

Now begin thinking about your Future in the next chapter.

5. YOUR FUTURE

"If you want to have something show up in your life . . .
you must first be able to imagine it."

—DR. WAYNE DYER, *WISHES FULFILLED*

"To put it simply, the formula for the good life is: living in the Place you
belong, with the people you Love, doing the right Work, on Purpose."

—RICHARD J. LEIDER AND DAVID A.

SHAPIRO, *REPACKING YOUR BAGS*

SEEING THE FUTURE HELPS make the future. What do you see for your-self? Do you already know exactly what you want in all areas of your life? If so, you are unusual. Odds are, even if you have some ideas for your future, a little or a *lot* of your vision is still fuzzy. The Life Map can help bring things into focus. These warm-up exercises may help get you started.

Warm-Up Exercises

Look for Role Models
Whom do you admire? Why? Do you know older people who seem happy or have led successful lives? Ask them how they did it. Is there anything they wish they'd known earlier?

_____

_____

_____

_____

Ask Yourself the Big Questions

What do I want to be known **as**: generous, creative, a loving parent, fun teacher, loyal friend, effective healer, hard worker, community organizer, entrepreneur, mentor, politician, talented cook, athlete, or other? What does being that person feel like?

_____

_____

_____

_____

What do I want to be known **for**: creating art, making people laugh, fighting poverty, serving my country, serving others, curing a disease, inventing or designing a new product, making people think about something in a new way, or something else? How will being known for that feel?

_____

_____

_____

_____

What parts of my life are most important to me in the future? Do I want to put my career first, my family first, or balance the two equally? Is my real passion—theater, music, charity work, sports, or other—my main job or do I pursue it in the after hours as part of my "play"? Do I still want to work part-time in retirement to keep active?

_____

_____

_____

_____

What do I need to have or to do in order to feel that I've had a successful life? Do I need to have had a happy marriage, close-knit family, children, lots of friends, one true friend, a certain amount of money, awards or recognition, spiritual understanding, or world travel? Do I need to have climbed Mount Everest, run a department or company, put my kids through college, taught a young person valuable skills, invented or cured something, or other?

_____

_____

_____

_____

What key values guide how I manage my relationships, my money, and my time? When I have difficult decisions or choices to make, what question or filter do I use? Are there credos or sayings that I live by?

_____

_____

_____

_____

Is there anything else I want to say about my "purpose" or "calling" in life (enjoy the ride, serve God, raise healthy children, save the rain forest)?

_____

_____

_____

_____

Go Wild

Believe, for just a moment, that anything is possible, that you have all the skills and resources to shape your life in any way you want. What would your most perfect life look like in two years, five years, or ten years? Imagine your relationships, job, health, home, and finances. Suspend worry about how realistic your fantasy is for now.

_____

_____

_____

_____

What of this fantasy do you insist on for your life? All of it? Parts of it? (Are you willing to do what it takes to be a Broadway star or would volunteering with a regional theater company satisfy you?)

_____

_____

_____

Make a Vision Board

This exercise taps into your intuition to express dreams for yourself. Vision Boards, also sometimes called Dream Boards, use words, images, and colors that you select to reflect your visions and desires for the future. They can be created virtually, by making a collage of digital photos you have or images you find online; or they can be made the old-fashioned way, by gluing magazine photos onto a poster board. When done, include elements of your vision in your Life Maps (e.g., if your Vision Board has a travel image of India, include a trip to India on your map).

Even if you're not inclined to create an actual Vision Board, at least go through the contemplative steps outlined on the next page. Do your best to "see" your creation. Store a mental picture of the results or even sketch it out on paper.

No two Vision Boards are alike. Yours can be as simple as a collage of magazine clippings that resonate with you, or it could include your own photos, words, and drawings. Your finished Vision Board will be a visual image that you can focus on as you set your daily, weekly, and monthly goals. Post it someplace where you'll see it every day.

If you're creating a paper Vision Board, you will need: a large sheet of sturdy paper or poster board; a photo of yourself (optional); a large pile of different kinds of magazines (with lots of photos); scissors; and rubber cement or a glue stick. If doing it on the computer, choose a program that allows you to insert images and move them around into a collage.

Step 1: (Optional) Place a photo that you like of yourself and that shows you feeling happy right in the middle of the board. There you are, deserving of a beautiful future.

Step 2: Sit quietly, with no distractions. Decide that all things are possible. Ask yourself what it is that you want to be, to do, to have, and to feel. What do you want to surround yourself with—what home, body, people, work, surroundings, toys? What makes you happy?

Step 3: Gather a collection of photos, images, colors, and words that delight you. Don't worry about fixing anything in place yet, just pick images using your intuition.

Step 4: Start laying your favorite images on the board. What feels right surrounding you? What doesn't? Sort the images by theme or lay them randomly, letting your gut tell you what to put closest to your photo.

Step 5: Give your Vision Board a title that inspires you. This might be the same title you choose later for your Whole-Life Map.

Done? What have you learned about your vision for the future? Display your board where you will see it every day—as your computer background if your board is digital, or someplace like your refrigerator door if your board is on paper.

_____

_____

_____

_____

Future Wants

List some specific elements that you want in your future, such as a farmhouse, your own restaurant, an Oscar statuette, two children, an abundant garden, leadership in your field, a best-selling novel, travel adventure, retirement by a lake, or other. These are the things you will be plotting out in your Life Maps.

MY FUTURE WANTS

Place

1.

2.

Family

1.

2.

Friends

1.

2.

Learning

1.

2.

Work

1.

2.

Service

1.

2.

Playing	1.	
	2.	
Other	1.	
	2.	

Writing Your Future

Read the questions below, listen to your thoughts, then write what speaks the loudest to you. If you need more space to answer, use a side notebook. After contemplating these questions, summarize your answers in the future maps, either with words or images. There won't be room in your maps for a lot of detail, just the most important points.

Have fun with this, and remember that you will not be a failure if what you write does not come true.

Years and Age: If you haven't already, fill out the years and your age along the top of the map. Optional: enter your death year and final age in your Whole-Life Map. Be generous; anticipate advances in human science, and a long, active life.

Place: Where do you see yourself living in the various time periods? Write the specific state, town, neighborhood, or home you will live in; describe the *kind* of region, town, neighborhood, or home (diverse, low-cost, yellow ranch); or express how the place you choose will feel (creative, energetic, safe).

_____

_____

Family: What family members do you see coming and going in your life? Will you have a life partner? Children? Grandchildren? What will be happening in their lives? Whom will you be close to? Are there family members who will need your attention or whose celebrations or challenges you want to be present for?

_____

_____

_____

_____

Friends: What friends or kinds of friends will you have? What kind of friend will you be? Who will be your support group or community? Will you be dating? What relationships will move to a primary role? What will be happening in significant friends' lives? If new friends will come into your life, how will you meet them (job, bridge club, neighborhood)? What social groups will you belong to?

_____

_____

_____

_____

Learning: What talents, skills, or knowledge will you be developing, either through work, formal schooling, casual classes, travel, hobbies, circumstance, online research, reading books, or other lifelong learning activities? This can include hard skills (accounting, first aid, tennis, writing), as well as soft skills (listening, forgiveness, gratitude, humor).

_____

_____

_____

_____

Work: What will your paid work be in the coming decades (if any)? Name the organizations, your positions or roles, the general fields or causes. What will your successes, rewards, or accomplishments be? Will you change jobs or careers entirely? What values or skills will you use? When will you retire, if at all?

_____

_____

_____

_____

Service: How do you want to make a difference in the future, and to whom or what—family, animals, nature, strangers in need, an organization or cause? Will you donate time or money? What will your role be (donor, teacher, mentor, caretaker, fund-raiser, advocate, builder, committee member)? Who will benefit? How?

_____

_____

_____

_____

Playing: What will you be doing—outside of work—that makes you happy? What hobbies and activities will entertain, nourish, excite, and relax you? Will these activities be a main source of your happiness or will other parts of your life be more important?

_____

_____

_____

_____

Other: Continue whatever themes you started in the past section of your map here (emotional highs and lows, financial milestones, world events, other) or start a new theme (fitness or financial goals, travel).

_____

_____

_____

_____

Ready to map out your future? Go now to your Subject Maps, your Ten-Year Map, or back to your Whole-Life Map and begin to sketch out the milestones, situations, structures, and images that you envisioned for yourself in this chapter for all the areas of your life. Use the chart on page 11 to help you decide what order to do the future maps in. Remember that your Whole-Life Map is the overview or long-term vision of your life, and the Ten-Year Map and Subject Maps are more detailed.

When done with fleshing out the future in your Whole-Life Map, create and name chapters for your future, just as you did earlier for your past.

Chapters: Group future years together into blocks of time that have a common theme. Give the chapters names ("Raising a Family," "Building Community," "Striking Gold," "Gone Fishing").

Life Title: Last but not least, give your life a title. Write it at the top of your Whole-Life Map. This is equivalent to the title of your autobiography, as if written at the end of your life. What captures the essence of your life journey? What do you want to be known for ("Just a Country Boy," "Someone Who Cared," "Creative Genius," "True Patriot," "Filled with Love")?

6. SUBJECT MAPS
The Next Ten Years

"Whatever your past has been, your future is spotless."

—ANONYMOUS

IN THIS SECTION YOU'LL be plotting out what you want various parts of your life—work, service, learning, family, friends, playing—to look like over the next ten years. Start with the subject that you are most comfortable with or that means the most to you. Each of these Subject Maps are summarized in one row of the consolidated Ten-Year Map in the next chapter.

1. Family

"Other things may change us, but we start and end with family."

—ANTHONY BRANDT

Create a ten-year plan for your family life, starting with your current age and year in the first column. (Each column is one year.)

Here are some warm-up questions to answer before creating your future family map.

Warm Up

If you could make one wish for a family member come true, what would it be, and for whom?

_____

_____

_____

Name one family member you admire or want to get to know better. What question do you want to ask him or her?

_____

_____

_____

Do you hope to add anyone to your family in the next ten years?

_____

_____

_____

What family member will need your help in the near future?

_____

_____

_____

Will any family members be celebrating a major milestone in the next ten years?

_____

_____

_____

MY TEN-YEAR FAMILY MAP

SUBJECT MAP: FAMILY					
DATE:					
YEARS					
AGE					
FAMILY OF ORIGIN (MOTHER, FATHER, BROTHERS, SISTERS)					
FAMILY OF CHOICE (LIFE PARTNER, CHILDREN, PETS)					
EXTENDED FAMILY (GRAND-PARENTS, AUNTS, UNCLES, COUSINS, IN-LAWS)					
OTHER (EXES, GOD-PARENTS, GOD-CHILDREN, OTHER)					

SUBJECT MAP: FAMILY

2. Friends

"Tell me who is your friend and I will tell you who you are."

—RUSSIAN PROVERB

*"You can make more friends in two months by becoming interested
in other people than you can in two years by trying to get other people
interested in you."*

—DALE CARNEGIE, *HOW TO WIN FRIENDS AND
INFLUENCE PEOPLE*

Create a ten-year plan for your friendships, starting with your current age and year
in the first column. (Each column is one year.) This map could include both platonic
and romantic (unmarried) relationships.

Here are some warm-up questions to answer before creating your future friends map.

Warm Up

What old friend would you like to reconnect with?

_____

_____

_____

_____

Do you prefer to do things with a big group of friends or just one or two close
friends?

_____

_____

_____

_____

What's the easiest way for you to make new friends?

_____

_____

_____

_____

What friend would you take with you on a vacation or special outing? Where would you go?

_____

_____

_____

_____

Describe a new friend that you hope to make in the next few years. How will you two meet?

_____

_____

_____

_____

MY TEN-YEAR FRIENDS MAP

SUBJECT MAP: FRIENDS					
DATE:					
YEARS					
AGE					
OLD FRIENDS TO KEEP (NAMES OR GROUPS)					
FRIENDS TO RECONNECT WITH OR DEEPEN (NAMES OR GROUPS)					
NEW FRIENDS TO MAKE, DATING LIFE (NAMES, TYPES, OR GROUPS)					
OTHER					

SUBJECT MAP: FRIENDS

3. Learning

"There are two types of education. One should teach us how to make a living, and the other how to live."

—JOHN ADAMS

"Let us think of education as the means of developing our greatest abilities, because in each of us there is a private hope and dream which, fulfilled, can be translated into benefit for everyone and greater strength for our Nation."

—JOHN FITZGERALD KENNEDY

Create a ten-year plan for learning, starting with your current age and year in the first column. (Each column is one year.)

Here are some warm-up questions to answer before creating your future learning map.

Warm Up

Are you already enrolled in any classes or programs? When will you finish?

_____

_____

_____

_____

Whom do you admire? Why? Is there anything you could learn or do in order to be more like them?

_____

_____

_____

_____

How do you learn best? Do you prefer using your eyes, ears, or hands to learn something new? Do you prefer studying alone or talking about it with a group?

_____

_____

_____

_____

What imaginary degree would you award yourself for something you will master in the next ten years (PhD in Barbecued Ribs, Master's in Soccer Coaching)?

_____

_____

_____

_____

MY TEN-YEAR LEARNING MAP

SUBJECT MAP: LEARNING

DATE:

YEARS					
AGE					
INFORMAL LEARNING (SUBJECT, SKILL, IDEA, LEARNING RESOURCES)					
FORMAL LEARNING (SCHOOL, DEGREE, TRAINING PROGRAM OR EVENT)					
OTHER					

SUBJECT MAP: LEARNING

4. Work

*"Be sure that, as you scramble up the ladder of success,
it is leaning against the right building."*

—STEPHEN COVEY

"Choose a job you love and you will never have to work a day in your life."

—CONFUCIUS

Create a ten-year plan for your work life, starting with your current age and year in the first column. (Each column is one year.)

Here are some warm-up questions to answer before creating your future work map.

Warm Up

What is one new skill you would love to try using at work?

_____

_____

_____

_____

What job in your current organization would you like to have (if any)?

_____

_____

_____

_____

What will your boss or clients praise you for in the next ten years?

_____

_____

_____

_____

Write the help wanted ad for your next job or assignment.

_____

_____

_____

_____

MY TEN-YEAR WORK MAP

SUBJECT MAP: WORK DATE:					
YEARS					
AGE					
EMPLOYER, GROUP, PLACE					
INDUSTRY OR FIELD					
JOB TITLE OR POSITION					
SKILLS OR TALENTS I USE					
MILE-STONES, SUCCESSES, MISSIONS					
TRAINING NEEDED					
REWARDS ($ OR OTHER)					
OTHER (LINKS TO LONG-TERM GOAL, CO-WORKERS)					

SUBJECT MAP: WORK

5. Service

"We make a living by what we get. We make a life by what we give."

—WINSTON CHURCHILL

"I alone cannot change the world, but I can cast a stone across the waters to create many ripples."

—MOTHER TERESA

Create a ten-year plan for serving others, starting with your current age and year in the first column. (Each column is one year.)

Here are some warm-up questions to answer before creating your future service map.

Warm Up

Whom or what do you most want to help in the next five to ten years?

_____

_____

_____

_____

If you could make one thing better for your family, community, or world, what would it be?

_____

_____

_____

_____

Do you generally prefer to donate time or money to solve problems? Why?

_____

_____

_____

_____

What would you consider a home run for your efforts in the next ten years?

_____

_____

_____

_____

MY TEN-YEAR SERVICE MAP

SUBJECT MAP: SERVICE					
DATE:					
YEARS					
AGE					
FOR MY FAMILY (ELDERS, CHILDREN, SIBLINGS, OTHERS)					
FOR MY LOCAL COMMUNITY (YOUTH, CLUB, CHARITY, TOWN, FAITH-BASED ORGANIZA-TION, CO-WORKERS)					
FOR MY GREATER COMMUNITY (EARTH, COUNTRY, NETWORK, GROUP, CAUSE, OTHER)					
OTHER					

SUBJECT MAP: SERVICE

6. Playing

"We do not stop playing because we grow old; we grow old because we stop playing."

—GEORGE BERNARD SHAW

"Live and work but do not forget to play, to have fun in life and really enjoy it."

—EILEEN CADDY

Create a ten-year plan for your recreational life, starting with your current age and year in the first column. (Each column is one year.)

Here are some warm-up questions to answer before creating your future play map.

Warm Up

When was the last time you had a deep belly laugh? What kinds of things make you laugh?

_____

_____

_____

_____

What would you like to learn how to do—just for fun—in the next ten years?

_____

_____

_____

_____

What is your favorite way to relax and forget your worries?

_____

_____

_____

_____

What places would you love to visit or travel to in the next ten years?

_____

_____

_____

_____

If you took a one week vacation at home (and weren't allowed to work or do unpleasant chores!), what would you do?

_____

_____

_____

_____

What is the best birthday gift you could imagine getting in the next ten years? For which birthday?

_____

_____

_____

_____

MY TEN-YEAR PLAYING MAP

SUBJECT MAP: PLAYING					
DATE:					
YEARS					
AGE					
PHYSICAL PLAY— DOING OR WATCHING (ACTIVITY, SPORT, LOCATION, PLAYMATES)					
CREATIVE PLAY (ART, CRAFTS, PERFORM- ING, DESIGNING, WRITING)					
MENTAL PLAY (GAMES, READING, PROJECTS)					
OTHER (TRAVEL, OTHER)					

SUBJECT MAP: PLAYING

7. TEN-YEAR MAP
All Subjects

"The best way to predict the future is to create it."

—PETER F. DRUCKER

N THE TEN-YEAR MAP, you imagine your medium-term future. If you've already done the Subject Maps, simply summarize each subject in this all-subject Ten-Year Map and see how all the parts of your vision fit together. If you are surprised by possible conflicts (starting medical school with a newborn), make adjustments. If you've already done your Whole-Life Map, use this Ten-Year Map to identify things you can do in the next ten years to move you toward your longer-term vision (training, reconciliations, experiences). An additional copy of the Ten-Year Map is offered in the back of the book (pages 102–103) for revisions at some point in the future.

Warm Up
Place: Describe your neighborhood or community in five years.

_____

_____

_____

Family: Name two significant events for your family over the next ten years (problem resolved, birth or death, relationship begun or ended, milestone met)?

_____

_____

_____

Friends: Who would you like to be better friends with or date? What relationships would you like to see evolve and grow or be eliminated?

_____

_____

_____

Learning: What new thing would you like to know how to do ten years from now (play the piano, learn Spanish, master a new technology, grow vegetables)?

_____

_____

_____

Work: What is the most fantastic thing you could imagine happening at work?

_____

_____

_____

Service: Thank yourself for helping this person, group, or cause in the next decade.

_____

_____

_____

Playing: What are two fun things on your ten-year "Must-Do" list?

_____

_____

_____

MY TEN-YEAR MAP

MY NEXT TEN YEARS DATE:					
YEARS					
AGE					
CHAPTER					
PLACE					
FAMILY					
FRIENDS					
LEARNING					
WORK					
SERVICE					
PLAYING					
OTHER					

8. WHOLE-LIFE

NAME:		**DATE:**	
YEARS			
AGE	0-20	21-30	31-40
CHAPTER			
PLACE			
FAMILY			
FRIENDS			
LEARNING			
WORK			
SERVICE			
PLAYING			
OTHER			

MAP

LIFE TITLE:			
41–50	**51–60**	**61–70**	**71–___**

9. PUTTING LIFE MAPS INTO PRACTICE

REFLECTIONS

"Go confidently in the direction of your dreams. Live the life you have imagined."

—HENRY DAVID THOREAU

"The future belongs to those who believe in the beauty of their dreams."

—ELEANOR ROOSEVELT

These next pages provide space for you to reflect on the journeys you mapped out and to record promises and affirmations for your future. You will also be invited to set three to five concrete goals for this year.

Questions you may want to ask yourself now are:

Which were the most difficult subjects or time periods to write about?

_____

_____

_____

Did the balance between family, work, play, friends, and other important areas of my life feel right?

_____

_____

_____

What did I learn from naming my life chapters?

_____

_____

_____

How did it feel to set my death date?

_____

_____

_____

Which parts of my future vision most excite me?

_____

_____

_____

Which parts will be easiest and hardest to achieve?

_____

_____

_____

Which parts of my vision do I need to talk through with key people in my life?

_____

_____

_____

Whom else should I talk to about my Life Map for moral support or coaching?

_____

_____

_____

Do I know someone else who would benefit from creating a Life Map?

_____

_____

_____

AFFIRMATION

Staying motivated and focused on your vision can be easier if you create a positive promise or affirmation to repeat again and again, such as: *I travel to exotic places*; *My loving nature attracts more love*; *I am a respected journalist*; *I choose to be rich*; *My marriage is built to last*; *I have the power to live my dream*; *I am prepared for success now*. Write an affirmation here that reinforces your future vision. Use the present tense.

_____

_____

_____

Other affirmations or reflections:

_____

_____

_____

_____

_____

_____

_____

_____

_____

_____

_____

←

NEXT STEPS— SETTING GOALS

"Motivation is when your dreams put on work clothes."

—BENJAMIN FRANKLIN

When you are done filling out your maps, don't just put the book on the shelf to collect dust. Find ways to start making things happen. Believe it, feel it, and commit to *three to five concrete goals for the next year* that move you toward your vision. Try to express these as **SMART** goals:

Specific: Say exactly what you will do in plain and simple words.

Measureable: Say how much, how many, how long.

Achievable: You have at least a 50-50 chance of accomplishing it within one year.

Relevant: It is in your Life Map or moves you toward a longer-term goal in your Life Map.

Timely: Say when you will start and finish this action.

SMART goals motivate because you know exactly what you need to meet them and you know when you made it. For example, let's say that you think getting in better physical shape is important to your goal of getting a better job. Setting a goal of "Get in shape" is too vague and too huge to know where to start. Better goals would be "Run a ten-minute mile by July 1" or "Go to the gym three times a week." They are specific, measureable, presumably achievable, relevant to your getting-in-shape goal (and your longer-term career goal), and they set a time frame.

What are three to five *SMART* goals you commit to doing over the next year that support your life vision?

This year I will:

_____

_____

_____

_____

_____

_____

_____

_____

Other suggestions for putting your Life Maps into practice:

☐ Copy your maps and display them as a daily reminder of where you are going.

☐ Talk about your maps with others—saying your dreams out loud make them more real.

☐ Do something every week that moves you toward these plans.

☐ Accept full responsibility for achieving these goals.

☐ Keep a note in your wallet, purse, calendar, phone, or anywhere else you frequently look that reminds you of your vision.

☐ Measure and celebrate progress often.

☐ *Believe* your plan, act on it now, and persist.

10. REMAPPING
Down the Road

"I can't change the direction of the wind, but I can adjust my sails to always reach my destination."

—JIMMY DEAN

"The art of life lies in constant readjustment to our surroundings."

—KAKUZŌ OKAKURA

LIFE IS INHERENTLY UNPREDICTABLE, so planning is a continual process. We are constantly adjusting and adapting to the actual results of our efforts, luck, fate, and fortune.

Every so often in the future, return to your maps. How often depends on you and your circumstances. Picking a regular schedule can work well. Come back to your maps every New Year's Day or on your birthday as part of an annual checkup ritual; when something unexpected (good or bad) has happened; when your circumstances have changed; or come back when you are unsatisfied with the path you're on and feel the need for an adjustment.

When you revisit your maps, see which of your plans have come true and which have not. Do you still want what you had set as your future? Has the time frame changed? Have new opportunities or challenges appeared? Have your priorities shifted?

Use this extra set of maps (Subject Maps, Ten-Year Map, and Whole-Life Map) for remapping at a later time. Digital versions of maps are available at www .marshallbooks.net (use code XM4U2MLM). Make a plan for remapping and mark it on your calendar.

My plan for remapping (how often, when, why):

_____

_____

_____

_____

_____

_____

_____

MY TEN-YEAR FAMILY MAP

SUBJECT MAP: FAMILY					
DATE:					
YEARS					
AGE					
FAMILY OF ORIGIN (MOTHER, FATHER, BROTHERS, SISTERS)					
FAMILY OF CHOICE (LIFE PARTNER, CHILDREN, PETS)					
EXTENDED FAMILY (GRAND-PARENTS, AUNTS, UNCLES, COUSINS, IN-LAWS)					
OTHER (EXES, GOD-PARENTS, GOD-CHILDREN, OTHER)					

SUBJECT MAP: FAMILY

MY TEN-YEAR FRIENDS MAP

SUBJECT MAP: FRIENDS DATE:					
YEARS					
AGE					
OLD FRIENDS TO KEEP (NAMES OR GROUPS)					
FRIENDS TO RECONNECT WITH OR DEEPEN (NAMES OR GROUPS)					
NEW FRIENDS TO MAKE, DATING LIFE (NAMES, TYPES, OR GROUPS)					
OTHER					

SUBJECT MAP: FRIENDS

MY TEN-YEAR LEARNING MAP

SUBJECT MAP: LEARNING					
DATE:					
YEARS					
AGE					
INFORMAL LEARNING (SUBJECT, SKILL, IDEA, LEARNING RESOURCES)					
FORMAL LEARNING (SCHOOL, DEGREE, TRAINING PROGRAM OR EVENT)					
OTHER					

SUBJECT MAP: LEARNING

MY TEN-YEAR WORK MAP

SUBJECT MAP: WORK DATE:					
YEARS					
AGE					
EMPLOYER, GROUP, PLACE					
INDUSTRY OR FIELD					
JOB TITLE OR POSITION					
SKILLS OR TALENTS I USE					
MILE-STONES, SUCCESSES, MISSIONS					
TRAINING NEEDED					
REWARDS ($ OR OTHER)					
OTHER (LINKS TO LONG-TERM GOAL, CO-WORKERS)					

SUBJECT MAP: WORK

MY TEN-YEAR SERVICE MAP

SUBJECT MAP: SERVICE					
DATE:					
YEARS					
AGE					
FOR MY FAMILY (ELDERS, CHILDREN, SIBLINGS, OTHERS)					
FOR MY LOCAL COMMUNITY (YOUTH, CLUB, CHARITY, TOWN, FAITH-BASED ORGANIZA-TION, CO-WORKERS)					
FOR MY GREATER COMMUNITY (EARTH, COUNTRY, NETWORK, GROUP, CAUSE, OTHER)					
OTHER					

SUBJECT MAP: SERVICE

MY TEN-YEAR PLAYING MAP

SUBJECT MAP: PLAYING DATE:					
YEARS					
AGE					
PHYSICAL PLAY— DOING OR WATCHING (ACTIVITY, SPORT, LOCATION, PLAYMATES)					
CREATIVE PLAY (ART, CRAFTS, PERFORM-ING, DESIGNING, WRITING)					
MENTAL PLAY (GAMES, READING, PROJECTS)					
OTHER (TRAVEL, OTHER)					

SUBJECT MAP: PLAYING

MY TEN-YEAR MAP

MY NEXT TEN YEARS DATE:					
YEARS					
AGE					
CHAPTER					
PLACE					
FAMILY					
FRIENDS					
LEARNING					
WORK					
SERVICE					
PLAYING					
OTHER					

MY WHOLE-LIFE MAP

YEARS			
AGE	0–20	21–30	31–40
CHAPTER			
PLACE			
FAMILY			
FRIENDS			
LEARNING			
WORK			
SERVICE			
PLAYING			
OTHER			

NAME:

DATE:

LIFE TITLE:

41–50	51–60	61–70	71-___

NOTES

_____
_____
_____
_____
_____
_____
_____
_____
_____
_____
_____
_____
_____
_____
_____
_____
_____
_____
_____
_____